TAKE THE LEAD *PLUS*

Bass Edition

D1193490

Jazz Standards

Series Editor: Chris Harvey

Editorial, production and recording: Artemis Music Limited • Design and production: Space DPS Limited • Published 2002

IMP

International MUSIC Publications

© International Music Publications Limited
Griffin House 161 Hammersmith Road London W6 8BS England

A Guide to Notation

Note and Rest Values
This chart shows the most commonly used note values and rests.

Name of note (UK)	Semibreve	Minim	Crotchet	Quaver	Semiquaver
Name of note (USA)	Whole note	Half note	Quarter note	Eighth note	Sixteenth note
Note symbol	o	♩	♩	♪	♪
Rest symbol	▬	▬	𝄽	𝄾	𝄿
Value per beats	4	2	1	1/2	1/4

Repeat Bars
When you come to a double dotted bar, you should repeat the music between the beginning of the piece and the repeat mark.

When you come to a repeat bar you should play again the music that is between the two dotted bars.

First, second and third endings
The first time through you should play the first ending until you see the repeat bar. Play the music again and skip the first time ending to play the second time ending, and so on.

D.C. (Da Capo)
When you come to this sign you should return to the beginning of the piece.

D.C. al Fine
When this sign appears, go back to the beginning and play through to the *Fine* ending marked. When playing a *D.C. al Fine*, you should ignore all repeat bars and first time endings.

D.S. (Dal Segno)
Go back to the 𝄋 sign.

D.S. al Fine
Go to the sign 𝄋 and play the ending labelled *(Fine)*.

D.S. al Coda
Repeat the music from the 𝄋 sign until the ⊕ or *To Coda* signs, and then go to the coda sign. Again, when playing through a *D. 𝄋 al Coda*, ignore all repeats and don't play the first time ending.

Accidentals
Flat ♭ - When a note has a flat sign before it, it should be played a semi tone lower.

Sharp ♯ - When a note has a sharp sign before it, it should be played a semi tone higher.

Natural ♮ - When a note has a natural sign before it, it usually indicates that a previous flat or sharp has been cancelled and that it should be played at its actual pitch.

Bar Numbers
Bar numbers are used as a method of identification, usually as a point of reference in rehearsal. A bar may have more than one number if it is repeated within a piece.

Pause Sign
A pause is most commonly used to indicate that a note/chord should be extended in length at the player's discretion. It may also indicate a period of silence or the end of a piece.

Dynamic Markings
Dynamic markings show the volume at which certain notes or passages of music should be played. For example

pp	= very quiet	*mf*	= moderately loud
p	= quiet	*f*	= loud
mp	= moderately quiet	*ff*	= very loud

Time Signatures
Time signatures indicate the value of the notes and the number of beats in each bar.

The top number shows the number of beats in the bar and the bottom number shows the value of the note.

TAKE THE LEAD*PLUS*

Introduction

Welcome to **Take The Lead *Plus*: Jazz Standards**, part of an instrumental series that provides all players with well-known songs and tunes as quartets. You will find that all parts have been arranged in a way that ensures playing any part is interesting and musically satisfying.

All eight pieces have been carefully selected and specially arranged to allow any number or combination of instruments to perform together using the other editions in the series – C, B♭ Brass, B♭ Woodwind, E♭ Brass and E♭ Woodwind.

The professionally recorded backing CD provides a complete demonstration performance, with all parts played over the backing track and an authentic accompaniment to play along with.

Also available is a Teachers' Edition which provides a four-part score (in C) for each of the arrangements and a piano accompaniment for use in rehearsal and performance. For increased involvement and added enjoyment, this edition also includes separate pull-out parts for both tuned and untuned percussion.

Wherever possible, we have simplified the more tricky rhythms. Also, we have kept marks of expression to a minimum, but feel free to experiment with these.

Above all, have fun and enjoy the experience of making music together.

Do Nothin' Till You Hear From Me

Demonstration

Backing

Words by Bob Russell
Music by Duke Ellington

Demonstration

Backing

It Don't Mean A Thing
(If It Ain't Got That Swing)

Words by Irving Mills
Music by Duke Ellington

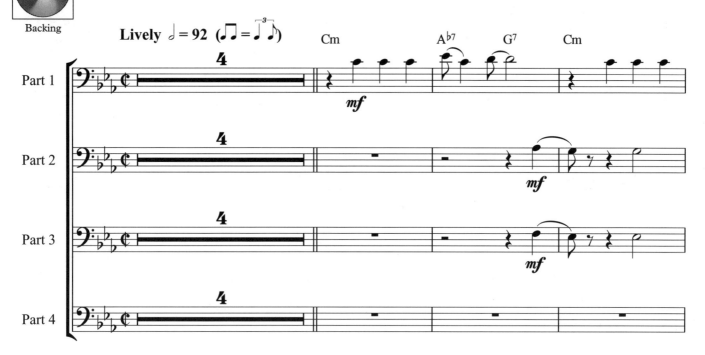

12

Misty

Music by Errol Garner

Demonstration

Backing

Jeepers Creepers

Words by Johnny Mercer
Music by Harry Warren

Whatever your instrument is...
you can now

TAKE THE LEAD *PLUS*

- Available in C, Bb, Eb and Bass Clef editions, this new concept opens up Take The Lead to a wider range of instruments, including cello, trombone, bassoon and baritone saxophone

- Flexible arrangements allowing players to team up with any number of instruments able to read from one of the 4 editions – C, Bb, Eb and Bass Clef.

- Each edition contains the full instrumental score in either 2,3 or 4 parts

- Professionally recorded backing tracks that re-create the sound of the original recordings.

TAKE THE LEAD

- Each book comes with a professionally recorded CD containing full backing tracks for you to play along with, and demonstration tracks to help you learn the songs

- Ideal for solo or ensemble use - in each edition, songs are in the same concert pitch key

- Each book includes carefully selected and edited top line arrangements; chord symbols in concert pitch for use by piano or guitar

- Suitable for intermediate players
  "A great way to get some relaxing playing done in between the serious stuff" **Sheet Music Magazine**

Discover The Lead

- This new 'spin off' of the Take The Lead series is ideal for beginners of all ages, grades 1-3

- The books contain simplified arrangements of well-known tunes to help the beginner develop reading and playing skills, while increasing confidence as a soloist

- Includes a useful fingering chart plus a CD with full backing and demonstration tracks

- Lots of helpful hints and technical tips to help you get to know your instrument

SHARE THE LEAD

- All pieces have been carefully selected and arranged at an easy level to provide fun material for today's instrumentalists

- All the arrangments work not only as duets for one particular instrument, but with all other instruments in the series (i.e. the flute book works with the clarinet book)

- The professionally recorded CD allows you to hear each song in 4 different ways – a complete demonstration of the track; part two plus backing so you can play along on part one; part one plus backing so you can play along on part two; and the backing only so you and a friend can Share The Lead!

Take The Lead

90s Hits
Air That I Breathe - I'll Be There For You - Something About The Way You Look Tonight - Frozen - How Do I Live - Angels - My Heart Will Go On - I Don't Want To Miss A Thing

Movie Hits
Because You Loved Me, Blue Monday, (Everything I Do) I Do It For You, I Don't Want To Miss A Thing, I Will Always Love You, Star Wars, The Wind Beneath My Wings

TV Themes
Coronation Street, I'll Be There For You (Theme from Friends), Match Of The Day, (Meet) The Flintstones, Men Behaving Badly, Peak Practice, The Simpsons, The X-Files

The Blues Brothers
She Caught The Katy And Left Me A Mule To Ride - Gimme Some Lovin' - Shake A Tail Feather - Everybody Needs Somebody To Love - The Old Landmark - Think - Minnie The Moocher - Sweet Home Chicago

Christmas Songs
Winter Wonderland - Little Donkey - Frosty The Snowman - Rudolph The Red Nosed Reindeer - Christmas Song (Chestnuts Roasting On An Open Fire) - Have Yourself A Merry Little Christmas - Santa Claus Is Comin' To Town - Sleigh Ride

Swing
Chattanooga Choo Choo - Choo Choo Ch'Boogie - I've Got A Gal In Kalamazoo - In The Mood - It Don't Mean A Thing (If It Ain't Got That Swing) - Jersey Bounce - Pennsylvania 6-5000 - A String Of Pearls

Jazz
Birdland - Desafinado - Don't Get Around Much Anymore - Fascinating Rhythm - Misty - My Funny Valentine - One O'Clock Jump - Summertime

Latin
Bailamos - Cherry Pink And Apple Blossom White - Desafinado - Guantanamera - La Bamba - La Isla Bonita - Oye Mi Canto (Hear My Voice) - Soul Limbo

Number One Hits
Believe, Cher - Careless Whisper, George Michael - Dancing Queen, Abba - Flying Without Wings, Westlife - I Will Always Love You, Whitney Houston - Livin' La Vida Loca, Ricky Martin - When You Say Nothing At All, Ronan Keating - You Needed Me, Boyzone

Classical Collection
Sheep May Safely Graze (Bach) - Symphony No. 40 in G Minor, 1st Movement (Mozart) - The Toreador's Song from Carmen (Bizet) - Hall Of The Mountain King from Peer Gynt (Grieg) - Radetzky March (Strauss) - Dance Of The Sugar Plum Fairy from The Nutcracker (Tchaikovsky) - Polovtsian Dances from Prince Igor (Borodin) - The Swan from Carnival of the Animals (Saint-Säens)

Rock 'n' Roll
Be-Bop-A-Lula - Blue Suede Shoes - Blueberry Hill - C'mon Everybody - Great Balls Of Fire - The Green Door - Jailhouse Rock - Let's Twist Again

Ballads
Amazed - Get Here - I Don't Want To Miss A Thing - A Little Bit More - My Heart Will Go On - The Rose - Swear It Again - The Wind Beneath My Wings

British Isles Folk Songs
All Through The Night - Greensleeves - The Leaving Of Liverpool - Loch Lomond - Men Of Harlech - Scarborough Fair - The Skye Boat Song - When Irish Eyes Are Smiling

Musicals
Fame – Food Glorious Food – If I Were A Rich Man – Over The Rainbow – Send In The Clowns – Singin' In The Rain – Tomorrow – Wouldn't It Be Lovely

Smash Hits
I'm Like A bird – It's Raining Men – Lady Marmalade – Out Of Reach – There You'll Be – Uptown Girl – The Way to Your Love – Whole Again

Grease
Beauty School Dropout – Greased Lightnin' – It's Raining On Prom Night – Look At Me, I'm Sandra Dee – Summer Nights – There Are Worse Things I Could Do – We Go Together – You're The One That I Want

Take The The Lead Plus

Pop Hits
Can't Fight The Moonlight – Bop Bop Baby – Hero – Hey Baby – How You Remind Me – It's OK – Just A Little – One Step Closer

Jazz Standards
Do Nothin' 'Till You Hear From Me - It Don't Mean A Thing (If It Ain't Got That Swing) - Jeepers Creepers - Misty - Moonlight In Vermont - On Green Dolphin Street - Stardust - The Shadow Of Your Smile

Share The The Lead

Chart Hits
Dancing Queen - Flying Without Wings - How Do I Live - Love's Got A Hold On My Heart - My Heart Will Go On - More Than Words - When You Say Nothing At All - You Needed Me

Film & TV Hits
Beautiful Stranger - Charlie's Angels - Don't Say You Love Me - I Believe - I'll Be There For You - Pure Shores - Searchin' My Soul - When You Say Nothing At All

Discover The Lead

Pop Hits
Don't Tell Me - Genie In A Bottle - Holler - Life Is A Rollercoaster - Millennium - Reach - Say What You Want - Seasons In The Sun

Classical Collection
Air On A G String (Bach) - Ave Maria (Schubert) - La Donna E Mobile from Rigoletto (Verdi) - Largo from New World Symphony (Dvorak) - Lullaby from Wiegenlied (Brahms) - Morning from Peer Gynt (Greig) - Ode To Joy from Symphony No. 9 (Beethoven) - Spring from The Four Seasons (Vivaldi)

Christmas Carols
Away In A Manger – The First Nowell – Hark! The Herald Angels Sing – O Come All Ye Faithful – O Little Town Of Bethlehem – Once In Royal David's City – Silent Night – We Three Kings Of Orient Are

Kids' Film & TV Themes
Animaniacs Theme – Can We Fix It? – Chitty Chitty Bang Bang – Hedwig's Theme – Number One – Over The Rainbow – Pokemon Main Theme – Scooby Doo Theme

Smash Hits
Anything Is Possible – Bop Bop Baby – Hero – Hey Baby – How You Remind Me – It's OK – Just A Little – One Step Closer

Moonlight In Vermont

Words by John Blackburn
Music by Karl Suessdorf

Track 10 Demonstration
Track 11 Backing

On Green Dolphin Street

Demonstration Backing

Words by Ned Washington
Music by Bronislaw Kaper

The Shadow Of Your Smile

Words by Paul Francis Webster
Music by Johnny Mandel

30

Star Dust

Demonstration　　Backing

Words by Mitchell Parish
Music by Hoagy Carmichael